RATTLESNAKES

Julie Murray

Big Buddy Books

An Imprint of Abdo Publishing
abdobooks.com

abdobooks.com

Published by Abdo Publishing, a division of ABDO, PO Box 398166, Minneapolis, Minnesota 55439.
Copyright © 2020 by Abdo Consulting Group, Inc. International copyrights reserved in all countries.
No part of this book may be reproduced in any form without written permission from the publisher.
Big Buddy Books™ is a trademark and logo of Abdo Publishing.

Printed in the United States of America, North Mankato, Minnesota
052019
092019

THIS BOOK CONTAINS
RECYCLED MATERIALS

Design: Sarah DeYoung, Mighty Media, Inc.
Production: Mighty Media, Inc.
Editor: Liz Salzmann
Cover Photograph: Shutterstock
Interior Photographs: iStockphoto (pp. 7, 8, 10–11, 19, 20, 25); Shutterstock (pp. 5, 12, 15, 16, 22, 23, 26–27, 29)

Library of Congress Control Number: 2018939644

Publisher's Cataloging-in-Publication Data
Names: Murray, Julie, author.
Title: Rattlesnakes / by Julie Murray.
Description: Minneapolis, Minnesota : Abdo Publishing, 2020. | Series:
    Animal kingdom | Includes online resources and index.
Identifiers: ISBN 9781532116513 (lib.bdg.) | ISBN 9781532158001 (ebook)
Subjects: LCSH: Rattlesnakes--Juvenile literature. | Snakes--Juvenile literature. |
    Snakes--Behavior--Juvenile literature. | Poisonous snakes--Juvenile literature.
Classification: DDC 597.9638--dc23

Contents

SNAKES ARE REPTILES

What do snakes, lizards, alligators, and turtles have in common? They are all **reptiles**.

Reptiles cannot make heat inside their bodies. They must find outside heat to warm themselves. Snakes and other **reptiles** lie in sunshine for warmth. Without this heat, reptiles become cold and slow moving.

Rattlesnakes lie in sunshine to warm themselves.

RATTLESNAKES

>>>>>>>

The rattlesnake is famous for its rattle. It shakes its rattle when danger is near. The rattle's sound warns others to stay away.

There are more than 30 kinds of rattlesnakes. These include the diamondback, the sidewinder, and the timber.

A sidewinder
rattlesnake

A rattlesnake's fangs stay hidden until it bites.

One kind of rattlesnake does not have a rattle. It is the Santa Catalina rattlesnake.

Rattlesnakes are pit **vipers**. Pit vipers have **venom** and hollow **fangs**. Venom is a poison. It makes the pit viper's bite deadly. The rattlesnake's bite can kill large animals.

SIZE AND COLOR

Most rattlesnakes are four to five feet (1 to 1.5 m) long. The eastern diamondback is the biggest rattlesnake. It can be seven feet (2 m) long. Adults weigh almost ten pounds (5 kg).

The eastern diamondback is the largest venomous snake in North America.

This rattlesnake's skin has a diamond pattern.

The **ridge**-nosed rattlesnake may be the smallest rattlesnake. Adults are between 12 and 24 inches (30 and 61 cm) long.

Most rattlesnakes are shades of brown or gray. Their skin often has patterns. Rattlesnakes may have stripes, **diamonds**, or circles.

BODY PARTS

The rattlesnake's rattle is on the end of its tail. It is made of **keratin**. Keratin is what a person's **fingernails** are made of.

A rattlesnake's rattle is also made of scales. Scales are flat **plates**. They cover **reptiles** all over. Snakes have special scales on their eyes too.

A rattlesnake shakes its rattle to warn predators.

A rattlesnake's pits
help it find prey.

Rattlesnakes and other pit **vipers** have two special pits. These pits are on the snake's head between its nose and eyes.

The pits help rattlesnakes sense heat. They can sense heat from nearby animals. This helps rattlesnakes find **prey**.

WHERE THEY LIVE

Most rattlesnakes live in western United States and Mexico. Southern Canada, Central America, and South America have rattlesnakes too. They live in deserts, mountains, **swamps**, **grasslands**, and forests.

A rattlesnake's coloring is often similar to its surroundings.

Rattlesnakes can't dig, so they may take over dens made by other animals.

Rattlesnakes **hibernate** in dens during the winter. A den is a hidden place. A rattlesnake's den may be a hole in the ground. Rattlesnakes often share their dens with other hibernating snakes. They leave their dens in the spring.

Tasting the Air

A snake "tastes" the air to understand its surroundings. First, it sticks out its tongue. Then, it wipes its tongue on two holes inside its mouth. These holes lead to the **Jacobson's organ**. The Jacobson's organ helps a snake taste what is on its tongue.

HUNTING AND EATING

Rattlesnakes only eat meat. They eat mice, frogs, lizards, squirrels, and other small animals.

Rattlesnakes use their special pits to find **prey**. They hide quietly and catch prey by surprise.

A rattlesnake can
strike in less than
half a second!

This rattlesnake is eating a rabbit.

Rattlesnakes quickly bite the **prey**. This sends **venom** into its body. The venom poisons and kills the prey.

Snakes can **stretch** their mouths very wide to eat. They swallow their food whole. Many snakes can eat animals that are wider than them!

RATTLESNAKE BABIES

Baby rattlesnakes grow inside their mothers. They grow inside eggs that do not have shells. Ten rattlesnakes may be born at one time.

Newborn rattlesnakes do not have rattles. They grow a part of the rattle every time they **shed** their skin.

Baby rattlesnakes have **venom**. They can hunt and feed themselves. Rattlesnakes can live for 25 years.

A baby rattlesnake

Glossary

diamond—a shape with four equal straight lines and in which each pair of opposite angles are different sizes.

fangs—long, sharp teeth.

fingernail—the hard covering at the end of a finger.

grassland—a large area of grass with few or no trees.

hibernate—to sleep or rest during the winter months.

Jacobson's organ—a special body part of snakes that helps them taste.

keratin—a fibrous protein found in fingernails, hair, feathers, hooves, claws, and horns.

plate—a thin, flat, stiff part or piece.

prey—an animal hunted or killed by a predator for food.

reptile—a member of a group of living beings. Reptiles have scaly skin and are cold-blooded.

ridge—a narrow, raised area on the surface of something.

shed—to cast aside or lose as part of a natural process of life.

stretch—to spread out to full size or greater.

swamp—land that is wet and often covered with water.

venom—a poison made by some animals and insects. It usually enters a victim through a bite or a sting. Something that has venom is venomous.

viper—a type of poisonous snake with long hollow fangs.

Online Resources

Booklinks
NONFICTION NETWORK
FREE! ONLINE NONFICTION RESOURCES

To learn more about rattlesnakes, please visit **abdobooklinks.com** or scan this QR code. These links are routinely monitored and updated to provide the most current information available.

Index